CHRISTOPHER COLUMBUS

CHRISTOPHER COLUMBUS

by Ann McGovern
Illustrated by James Watling

SCHOLASTIC INC.

New York Toronto London Auckland Sydney

ISBN 0-590-45765-9

Text copyright © 1962 by Ann McGovern.
Illustrations copyright © 1992 by Scholastic Inc.
All rights reserved. Published by Scholastic Inc.

12 11 10 9 8 7 6   8 9/9 0 1 2/0

Printed in the U.S.A.   23

First Scholastic printing, September 1992

CHRISTOPHER COLUMBUS

For another brave
explorer named Christopher —
Christopher Mulligan.

Long, long ago there lived a small boy who loved the sea more than anything else.

He loved the smell of the salty sea.

He loved to watch the ships come and go.

"Someday I will sail across the sea," he said to his younger brother, Bartholomew. "I will sail across the sea to new lands."

What big dreams for such a little boy!

"Christopher Columbus!" his mother scolded. "You are a weaver's son. But do you weave cloth? Oh, no! You weave dreams. Dreams of the sea — that's what you weave."

The town in Italy where Christopher Columbus grew up was called Genoa. Along the waterfront of Genoa, many ships were built. And from the harbor, ships sailed to faraway lands.

Almost every day, Columbus worked in his father's shop preparing the wool for weaving. When his work was done, he hurried down to the harbor to watch the shipbuilders, sailors, and fishermen. Or he went to the shops of the town where maps were made and sold.

The sailors, fishermen, and mapmakers liked the blue-eyed boy with red hair and freckles. Sailors told him stories of their adventures.

Fishermen took him along with them on their fishing boats at night.

Mapmakers showed him maps of lands he dreamed about.

When Columbus lived, about 500 years ago, people did not know as much about the world as we do today. Many people thought the world was flat, shaped like a saucer or a pancake.

They said, "If a ship sailed to the edge of the world, it would fall off and be lost forever."

They spoke of oceans boiling hot. They spoke of dragons waiting to eat sailors who dared to sail so far. They spoke of terrible dangers in the ocean they called the Sea of Darkness.

But many sea captains and men of learning said the world was not shaped like a pancake. They said the world was round, like an orange.

Columbus thought so, too. He studied maps and charts. He tried to learn all he could about the size and shape of the world.

He watched the ships sail in and out of the harbor. He listened to the talk of sailors. But watching and listening were not enough. Columbus longed to sail on a ship himself.

One day, when Columbus was about fourteen years old, his father said, "There is a ship sailing soon. It will bring back wine and wool and cheese. Would you like to be on that ship?"

Would he! There was no happier boy in all of Genoa. His first voyage! And although it was a short one, Columbus remembered it all his life.

He made many more trips along the coast to other towns in Italy.

Each time he sailed he learned something new.

He learned how to handle the sails and masts and ropes.

He learned how to use a compass.

He learned what to do when the wind blew too hard or when there was no wind at all.

After each exciting voyage it seemed harder than ever to work in the weaving shop. And when he was twenty-two, Columbus left the shop for good. From now on he would be a sailor. And a sailor's dream began to grow.

Columbus heard sailors speak of lands in the Far East. Their very names seemed magical: Cipangu and Cathay. And they spoke of India, land of spices.

Columbus heard the sailors speak of a traveler called Marco Polo, who had visited these lands almost 200 years before. Marco Polo had written a book about his adventures. In his book, he wrote of the wonders he had seen. He wrote of temples with roofs of gold. He wrote of heaps of jewels, and of spices growing all over the land.

Marco Polo had traveled across mountains and deserts to get to the Far East. It was a long voyage by land. In Columbus's day, enemies of Spain controlled these lands. Men looked for a new way to go by sea. They thought the only way to reach the Far East was to sail all around the coast of Africa.

Columbus thought there must be a shorter way. The world was really round. Of this he was sure. Then couldn't he sail west to reach the east?

As a sailor, Columbus made many voyages. One voyage almost turned out to be his last. He was sailing near the coast of Portugal. Suddenly his ship was attacked by pirates. The pirates and the sailors fought all day. The ship caught on fire and began to sink. Many sailors jumped into the sea.

Columbus jumped, too. But he had hurt his leg. He

could not swim to shore, and now it was dark.

A broken mast drifted by. Columbus reached for it. Now he could paddle awhile, then rest awhile on the floating wood.

Hours passed. No help came. His leg hurt terribly. All night he held on to the wooden mast and paddled toward shore.

In the morning, fishermen dragged him out of the water. Later they told him he was not far from the city of Lisbon.

For a moment Columbus forgot the terrible pain in his leg.

Lisbon! he thought. God is good to bring me so close to the greatest port in the world.

In Lisbon he could learn.

He could learn Portuguese — to speak the language of sailors.

He could learn Latin — to read the works of learned men.

In Lisbon, there were many shops where maps were made. There were great ships in the harbor. The captains talked of new lands they had seen. They talked of new lands to be discoverd and explored.

In Lisbon, Columbus studied. He began to think more and more of sailing west to reach the lands in the Far East — of sailing out on the Sea of Darkness.

The years he spent in Lisbon were happy ones. His brother, Bartholomew, was there, too. He was a good mapmaker. The brothers made maps and sold them in their own shop. From Lisbon, Columbus made more voyages.

When he was twenty-eight, Columbus married a girl from a noble family. She was a captain's daughter. A year later a son was born to them. They named him Diego.

By this time Columbus felt he had been away from sea too long. His dream was still with him. He was more certain than ever that he could reach the Indies by sailing west.

Now Columbus wanted to make his dream come true.

To do this, he would need ships and a crew of men to sail them. The voyage would cost much money. He would ask the King of Portugal for help.

Would the King believe in his plan? Would he give him the money? Columbus said good-bye to his wife and baby son and set out for the King's court.

Columbus told King John, "Let me have ships, and men to sail them. The lands I find beyond the Sea of Darkness will belong to Portugal. Your country will become rich with gold and spices from the Far East."

King John told Columbus to leave his maps and charts. "My men will study them. They will tell me if your plan is good."

Columbus waited for months and months.

One day he learned the reason for the long wait. And what he heard he could hardly believe! The King had tricked him. He had used Columbus's maps and charts. He had sent one of his own captains to sail the very route Columbus had planned so carefully.

It was lucky for Columbus that the voyage failed. The captain was afraid to sail too far on the Sea of Darkness.

But now Columbus knew he could never trust King John again.

These were sad days for Columbus. And the days became even sadder when he learned that his wife had died.

Columbus took his five-year-old son, Diego, to Spain. He left him in the kind care of some monks and went to see King Ferdinand and Queen Isabella of Spain. Perhaps they would listen to his plan and believe in it.

But the King and Queen said they had to think about the plan. A voyage like that would cost so much! And Spain was at war. There was no money for ships and sailors.

So once more Columbus waited. He waited for weeks, for months, for years. Columbus was only thirty-five years old, but his long red hair had already turned white.

These years of waiting were hard for Columbus. His wife was dead. His son could not be with him.

But there were some happy times, too. He met
men at court who believed in his dream. He met a
woman he grew to love. And in 1488 his second son,
Ferdinand, was born.

Spain was still at war. To make sure the King and
Queen did not forget him, Columbus followed them
to the battlefields.

Meanwhile, Bartholomew went to England and
France to seek help for his brother.

Year followed year. There were people who
thought Columbus was crazy. They said, "There is no
end to the Sea of Darkness. The King and Queen
will never listen to your plan."

Six years had passed since Columbus first saw
King Ferdinand and Queen Isabella. He would wait
no longer. He would go to France.

Columbus left the court. He stopped to visit his son Diego, who was now eleven years old. Columbus told his story to the good monks who were taking care of Diego. One of the monks, Father Perez, begged Columbus not to go to France. He promised to help him. Father Perez knew the Queen. He wrote to her. Would she be willing to see Columbus once more?

Queen Isabella wrote back right away. Yes, she would see Columbus. She even sent money so he could buy new clothes and a mule.

So once more, Columbus stood before the King and Queen. This time they said yes to his plan.

They would give him money for his voyage.

Now Columbus told them what he wanted for his reward.

He wanted an important title. He wanted to be called Admiral of the Ocean Sea.

He wanted to be in charge of any new lands he discovered.

And he wanted to share in the gold, silver, pearls, gems, spices, and all other riches of these new lands.

The King and Queen stared at Columbus. Who was he to ask for so much? He was only an unknown sailor. They took back their offer to help him.

Columbus left the court — forever, he thought. He had never been so angry. As he rode away on his mule, he said to himself, "I was right not to give in. I worked so hard. I waited so long. Yes, what I asked for was right! I will never go back to . . ."

Suddenly he heard hoofbeats. He turned. The man on the galloping horse was a messenger from the Queen. He had orders to bring Columbus back. The Queen had changed her mind.

And so the long wait was over.

What lay ahead? Adventure. Discovery.

And the unknown Sea of Darkness.

There wooden ships were made ready. It would take ninety men to sail them. But who would want to sail over an unknown ocean? Most sailors thought the world was flat. They did not want to sail off the edge of the world and be eaten by sea monsters.

How could Columbus get sailors for his ships? The King's soldiers forced some men to sign up. He got four more from the town jail. These men had their choice. They could rot in jail, or they could sail with Columbus. They decided to take a chance with Columbus.

Some of the crew were young boys seeking adventure.

Some were old sailors seeking gold.

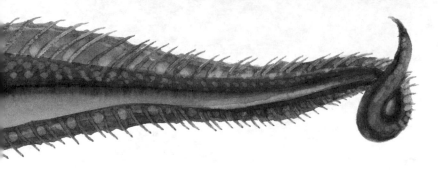

Columbus made sure he had skilled men, too. There were doctors, carpenters, and able seamen.

At last everything was ready.

On board was a chest heaped with trinkets for trading with the natives. There were glass beads and red caps, mirrors and brass bells. Great casks of water and wine were shipped aboard. There was enough salted meat and fish, cheese, and biscuits to last a year.

On the third day of August, in the year 1492, Christopher Columbus set sail from the port of Palos, Spain. Three small wooden ships — the *Niña*, the *Pinta*, and the *Santa María* — sailed out for an unknown sea.

Columbus kept a diary, or log, of the voyage. Each day, he wrote how far he had sailed, what he had seen, and what had happened.

On the third day at sea the rudder of the *Pinta* broke loose. They had to stop at one of the Canary Islands for repairs.

On September 6, the men saw fire and smoke rising from the top of a tall mountain. They were so frightened, they wanted to turn back at once. In a calm voice, Columbus told them that this was a volcano. He told them there was nothing to fear.

By September 9, they had sailed out of sight of land. For days they sailed. For weeks they sailed.

Never before had they sailed so long without seeing land.

Most of the men were afraid.

"Turn back," they begged Columbus. "Turn back before the sea dragons eat us."

But Columbus was not afraid. He knew there were no sea dragons.

He tried to cheer up the sailors. He told them of the gold that would soon belong to them. He told them the King would give a lot of money to the first man who saw land.

But the men muttered and grumbled. The men grumbled when the wind blew too hard. They grumbled when there was no wind at all. And they grumbled about the weeds they saw in the sea.

"Many bunches of very green weed," Columbus wrote in his log on September 16.

Some of the men were afraid the ships would get stuck in the thick green and yellow weeds. Columbus said the ships would sail right through. And they did.

On the night of September 25, a shout came from the *Pinta*. "Land! Land, sir! The reward is mine!"

The men climbed up the rigging. Everyone shouted that he saw land.

Columbus fell to his knees and thanked God.

That night no one slept. But in the morning, there was no land.

What they had thought to be land was only a low cloud. Columbus wrote in his log: "What had supposed to be land was not, but sky."

That day the men were more angry than ever. They said, "There is not much drinking water left. We will die of thirst."

"Let's throw Columbus overboard."

"We could say he fell in."

Columbus heard the men plotting.

He told them, "Kill me if you like. But it will do you no good. The King and Queen will hang every last one of you if you come home without me."

Then he reminded them that the first man to sight land would get a reward. "And I myself will give a fine jacket of silk," he said.

But these words did not comfort the frightened sailors. They kept their knives handy. They were ready to kill.

By October 10, even the captains of the *Pinta* and the *Niña* asked Columbus to turn back.

Columbus thought, Land is near. I'm sure of it. But how can I make my men believe it?

He begged them, "Give me three days. Only three days. If we do not see land by that time, I promise we shall sail home."

All day Columbus watched for land.

Suddenly a flock of birds flew overhead. A branch with shiny leaves and pink flowers floated by. Land must be near!

Now there was no more talk of turning back. Now the sailors watched eagerly for the first sight of land.

On the night of October 11, one hour before moonrise, Christopher Columbus thought he saw a light. Later he wrote it was like "a little wax candle rising and falling."

One minute he saw it.

The next minute it was gone.

Columbus stood on the deck for four hours watching and waiting.

The moon was bright. And the sails looked as if they were made of silver.

It was two o'clock in the morning of October 12, 1492.

Suddenly a cry was heard in the quiet night: "Land! Land ahead!"

Christopher Columbus looked. He saw a sandy beach gleaming in the moonlight. And behind the beach was a forest of tall palm trees.

The voyage was over. It had taken sixty-nine days.

Quickly, Columbus dressed in his best clothes. He put on his armor and threw a red cloak over his shoulders. As soon as it was light enough, the men lowered the rowboats.

A few minutes later, Columbus stood on the soil of a new land. He knelt to kiss the ground.

As he gave thanks to God, tears of joy streamed down his face. He rose and planted the flag of Spain in the new land. He called the island San Salvador.

There were many natives on the island. Columbus called the natives "Indians" because he was sure San Salvador was near India. He saw that the Indians were gentle and friendly. Later he wrote, "The Indians are well made, of very handsome bodies and very good faces. Some paint themselves black, some paint themselves white, and others red."

Where were their great cities? Where were the palaces with roofs of gold?

The only gold Columbus found on San Salvador were thin golden rings the natives wore in their noses and ears. In exchange for this gold, Columbus and his men traded glass beads and red caps and brass bells.

Columbus and the Indians could not speak each other's language. They used sign language. The Indians told them that the gold came from farther south.

For almost two weeks the men of the *Niña*, the *Pinta*, and the *Santa María* sailed, looking for gold. They found many beautiful islands. They found strange birds and fish and natives everywhere.

But they did not find gold.

On October 28, they reached the large island of Cuba. Columbus wrote in his log: "It was a great pleasure to see green things and groves of trees and to hear the birds sing."

But the King and Queen of Spain had not asked Columbus to bring back trees and singing birds. They wanted riches for Spain.

Columbus and his men kept on looking for gold. They came to the beautiful island of Haiti on December 6. Columbus named it Hispaniola.

More than a thousand natives visited the ships. Some came in boats. Others swam. They brought many presents for Columbus. They gave him fruit, cotton, and parrots. But it was the pieces of gold they brought that made Columbus the most happy.

Now he was sure there was a rich gold mine on Hispaniola.

Christmas was only a few days away. Perhaps he would find the gold mine by then. What a wonderful Christmas that would be!

It was Christmas Eve, one hour before midnight. The new moon cast a pale light on two ships. The *Niña* was well ahead of the *Santa María*. The captain of the *Pinta* had sailed his ship away weeks before.

Almost all of the men aboard the *Santa María* were fast asleep. For the first time in two days, Columbus slept, too.

The officer in charge rubbed his eyes and yawned. He thought, There is no sign of wind. This is a good chance to get some rest.

He ordered the ship's boy to take charge.

"Call me if the wind changes," the officer said. Then he, too, fell asleep.

The sleepy ship's boy was the only one awake.

And just at midnight, as Christmas Day began, the *Santa María* slid gently onto a coral reef. This happened so quietly that no one on the ship awoke until the ship's boy called for help. But it was too late.

Waves lifted the wooden ship higher and higher. The rock reef split it to pieces.

The ship was wrecked beyond repair.

That was the end of the *Santa María* — the ship that had carried Columbus on his long voyage.

No one knew where the *Pinta* was.

Only the *Niña* was left. How could all the men sail home on that one little ship?

And what about the gold that Columbus felt sure was somewhere on Hispaniola?

Columbus made up his mind. He would build a fort on the island from the wood of the *Santa María*. He would leave some men behind to find the gold mine.

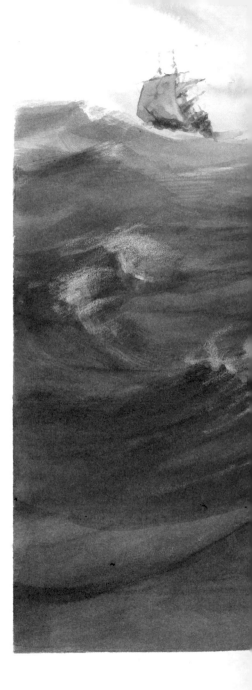

So the first fort was built in the new land. Columbus called it *La Navidad*, the Spanish word for Christmas.

On January 4, the little *Niña* began the voyage home. The men on board were happy. They had trinkets and parrots and bits of gold to show off when they reached Spain.

Two days later the crew of the *Niña* saw the missing *Pinta*. Now the *Niña* would have company for the long voyage ahead.

After six weeks of sailing, the *Niña* and the *Pinta* ran into a fearful storm. Once more the *Pinta* sailed away. Once more the *Niña* was alone.

Lightning flashed. Angry waves swept over the decks of the little *Niña*. Everything that was not tied down rolled and clattered about the decks and the cabins. The *Niña* tossed and pitched in the stormy seas.

Columbus was just as frightened as his men. What if the *Niña* went to the bottom of the sea? What if the captain of the *Pinta* claimed all the glory for himself? What would happen then to his young sons, Ferdinand and Diego? They must have their share of glory, too.

While the storm raged, Columbus wrote a letter to the King of Spain. He told him of all the islands he had discovered. He told him of the gold he had found. He wrapped the letter in a waxed cloth and put it into a wooden barrel and threw it into the sea.

The letter never reached shore. But Columbus and his crew arrived safely at the port of Palos, Spain, on March 15, 1493. The *Pinta* arrived the same day. The entire voyage had taken thirty-two weeks — almost eight months.

There was no greater hero in the land than Christopher Columbus. Everywhere he went, great crowds lined the way.

"There is the man who sailed to the Indies and back!" they shouted.

"There is the man who found gold!"

The King and Queen sent for him. They addressed their letter to the Admiral of the Ocean Sea. They asked him to hurry to their court at Barcelona. And they asked him to prepare for another voyage as soon as possible.

At Barcelona, all the city and the court came out to meet the great Admiral.

Flags flew. Bands played.

Columbus knelt before the King and Queen. But they made him rise and take a place beside them. This was his proudest moment!

King Ferdinand and Queen Isabella listened to the story of his travels. They looked at all the wonders he had brought back — the ten Indians, the parrots, cotton, fruit and plants, stones and shells. And they looked at the gold. There was not much, but it was gold just the same.

Columbus was already making plans for his next voyage. "This time," he told the Queen, "I will sail past the islands of the Indies. I will reach the mainland of China, Japan, and India. And I will bring back much more gold."

But he never did.

Columbus made three more voyages. He reached different parts of the Americas. Each time, he thought he was sailing to the Indies. But he never found the palaces with roofs of gold. And although he found some gold, it was not enough to please the King and Queen.

They took some of his titles away from him. He was not allowed to rule the lands he found. And although he was not a poor man, he did not have great riches to leave to his sons. When Columbus died at the age of fifty-four, he was a disappointed man.

Christopher Columbus made four voyages. All his life he was sure he had reached the Far East. He was sure he had reached the lands near China and Japan and India. He never knew that he had found a whole new land instead.

How do we know about Columbus?

Columbus lived so long ago. How do we know what he was really like? How do we know what really happened 500 years ago?

There are some things about Columbus we will never know.

There are some things we know for sure.

There are some things people are still arguing about.

How do we know what Columbus looked like? How do we know what he did, and what he thought?

Well, museums and libraries have some of the letters that Columbus wrote. There are maps that Columbus and other people made. These maps show what they thought the world was like. There are paintings that show how people dressed.

We have Columbus's own words in the log, or diary, he kept.

Some of the very things Columbus said have been used in this book. He did not write in English, of course. He wrote in Spanish.

Columbus's son Ferdinand wrote a book about his

father. And a friend wrote a book about Columbus soon after he died. But people who knew Columbus did not always say the same things about him. They did not always agree.

In his book, Ferdinand wrote about the way King John tried to trick Columbus. He told how King John gave the maps Columbus had made to another man. But some people said Columbus's son did not understand what really happened. We may never know for sure.

We do know what Columbus looked like. Everyone who knew Columbus and wrote about him spoke of his red hair and his blue eyes. They all agreed that he was tall and stood very straight.

We know where Columbus went on his voyages. We can tell from the maps and notes he made where he really landed. He landed on islands in the Bahamas, the Caribbean, and in Central America. And though he later went to South America, he never landed on North America. Some people say that Christopher Columbus "discovered" America. But there were many thousands of Indians already living on the lands Columbus wandered into by mistake. The Indians had their own proud culture long, long before Columbus was born.

There are men and women who try to find out about what happened in the past. They look for old letters and old maps. They study the paintings and writings made by people long ago. They are called *historians*.

And because of them, authors can learn the things they need to know so they can write a book like this one.